YOUNG DISCOVERERS

NATURE IN DANGER

ROSIE HARLOW & SALLY MORGAN

**KING*fisher*
NEW YORK**

KINGFISHER
Larousse Kingfisher Chambers Inc.
80 Maiden Lane
New York, New York 10038
www.kingfisherpub.com

First American edition published in 1995
10 9 8 7 6 5 4 3 2 1

1TR/1201/WKT/- (RNB)/128MA

LIBRARY OF CONGRESS CATALOGING-IN-
PUBICATION DATA
Harlow, Rosie.
Nature in danger / Rosie Harlow,
Sally Morgan.—1st ed.
p.   cm.—(Young discoverers)
Includes bibliographical references and index.
1. Nature conservation—Juvenile literature.
2. Ecology—Juvenile literature 3. Habitat
(ecology)—Juvenile literature.
[1. Conservation of natural resources.
2. Ecology. 3. Habitat (Ecology)]
I. Sally Morgan. II. Title. III. Series.
QH75. H367   1995
333.9516—dc20 95-6368 CIP AC

ISBN 0-7534-5504-8

Editor: Jilly MacLeod
Designer: Shaun Barlow
Photo research: Elaine Willis
Cover design: John Jamieson and
    Shaun Barlow
Illustrations: Peter Bull p. 5 (top), 13 (bot.),
    15, 21 (right), 25, 29 (bot. right),
    31 (top); John Butler p. 28; Richard
    Draper p. 8 (right); Angelika Elsebach
    p. 8 (left), 12, 18 (left and top), 22 (left
    and top), 24 (top); Deborah Kindred
    p. 27 (right); Ruth Lindsay p. 4-5 (bot.),
    26-27 (bot.), 27 (top left), 29 (left and
    top); Eric Robson p. 6, 7 (bot.), 14,
    20-21; Mike Saunders p. 16 (bot.), 22
    (bot. right); Richard Ward p. 7 (top), 10
    (left), 11 (bot.), 16 (top), 17, 18-19
    (bot), 23; Ann Winterbotham cover,
    p. 9, 10-11, 13 (top), 24 (left), 30,
    31 (bot.)
Photographs: Ecoscene p. 6 (W. Lawler),
    9 (N. Hawkes), 12 (E. Schaffer), 19
    (N. Hawkes); Greenpeace p. 26
    (Morgan); NHPA p. 14 (B. Jones and
    M. Shimlock), 15 (D. Woodfall), 17
    (R. Tidman), 25 (M. Wendler), 28;
    Oxford Scientific Films (L. Lee Rue) p. 21.

Printed in Hong Kong

About This Book

This book looks at the world of nature and explains how we are destroying habitats and harming wildlife by the way we live. It suggests lots of experiments and things to look out for, as well as ways we can all help to protect plants and animals.

You should be able to find nearly everything you need for the experiments in your home, or in a backyard, park, or nearby woods. Be sure to put any wild creatures back where you found them after you have finished an experiment.

Activity Hints

● Before you begin an experiment, read through the instructions carefully and collect all the things you need.

● When you have finished, clear everything away, especially sharp scissors, and wash your hands.

● Start a special notebook so you can keep a record of what you do in each experiment and the things you find out.

Contents

Where Animals Live

Plants and animals are found almost everywhere on Earth—in the air, on the land, underground, and in the water. Each living thing belongs to a particular kind of place, called its habitat. For example, cacti grow in the desert, jellyfish are found in the sea, and parrots live in tropical forests. When people cut down trees to make way for roads and farms or pour harmful chemicals into the environment, they damage these habitats and destroy the wildlife.

There are many different types of habitat in the world, from the tropical rain forests to the polar ice caps. This picture shows the kinds of animal that live in some of these habitats.

Reefs at Risk

Coral reefs are home to many sea creatures and plants. Unfortunately, they are threatened by people who are polluting the oceans and damaging their habitat.

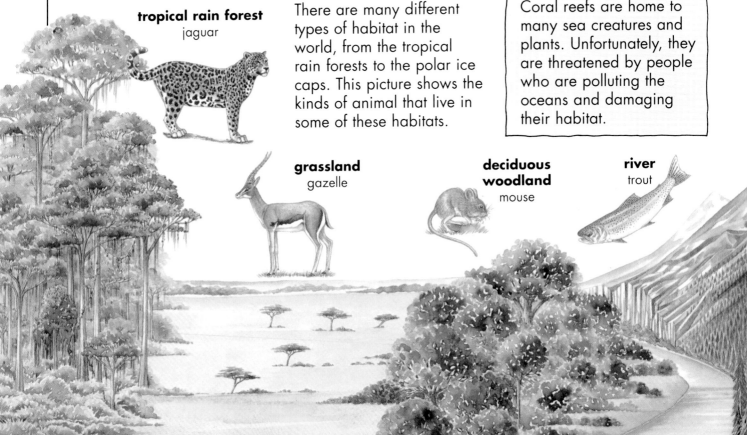

tropical rain forest
jaguar

grassland
gazelle

deciduous woodland
mouse

river
trout

Do it yourself

Find out what type of habitat wood lice like best.

1. First, find some wood lice by looking under logs and bark.

2. Then spread a thin layer of cotton batting onto a small tray or box lid. Number the four corners of the tray with labels as shown here.

3. Cover half the tray with newspaper while you spray areas 1 and 2 with water. The batting should be damp but not soaking wet.

4. Lay a piece of black paper cut to size over areas 1 and 3.

5. Now put your wood lice in the middle of the tray and see which area they go to.

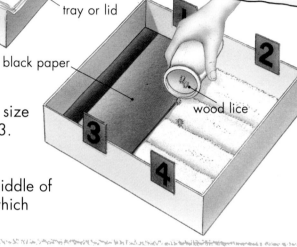

water spray

cotton batting

newspaper

tray or lid

black paper

wood lice

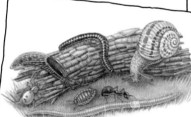

How It Works

You have divided the tray into four areas—(1) dark and damp, (2) light and damp, (3) dark and dry, and (4) light and dry. Wood lice prefer dark, damp habitats, so they will go to area 1.

mountain
eagle

coniferous forest
wolf

ocean
whale

polar regions
polar bear

👁 Eye-Spy

If you want to see some animals in their natural habitat, turn over a log in your yard or local park. How many different creatures can you find?

Keeping the Balance

Plants and animals that share the same habitat rely on each other for their survival. A delicate balance exists between them which depends largely on the amount of food available. Plants are able to make their own food, but animals have to find ready-made food. Some animals only eat plants—they are called herbivores. Other animals feed off the plant-eaters. These are the carnivores, or meat-eaters. But the balance is easily upset. For example, if fishermen catch too many sand eels, the seabirds that feed on the eels may die because they have no more food.

People upset the balance of nature when they cut down large areas of forest. The animals whose lives depend on the trees for food and shelter soon die.

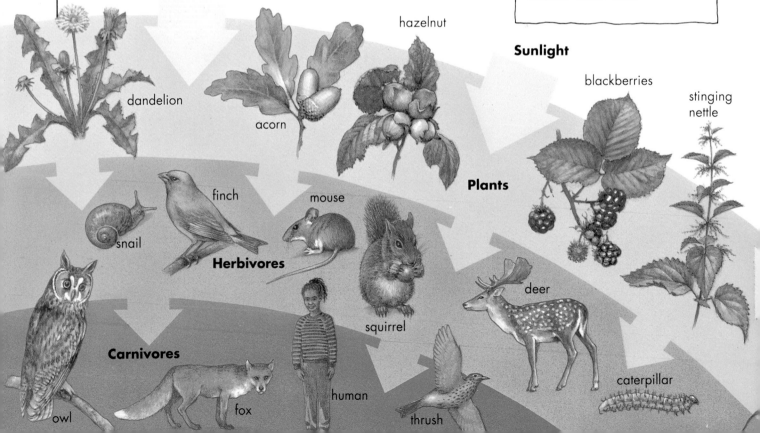

hazelnut

Sunlight

dandelion

acorn

blackberries

stinging nettle

Plants

finch

mouse

snail

Herbivores

squirrel

deer

Carnivores

human

owl

fox

thrush

caterpillar

Do it yourself

See a food chain in action.

1. Find a small leafy shoot that has a few aphids on it. (Try looking on roses or nasturtiums.) Put the shoot into a small bottle of water and plug the mouth of the bottle with tissue paper.

2. Put the bottle in a large glass jar. Cover the top with thin woven fabric—from an old handkerchief or a pair of panty hose. Use a rubber band to hold it in place.

3. Watch the aphids for a few days through a magnifying glass. Can you see them sucking juices out of the plant?

4. Now put a ladybug into the jar and watch it feed on the aphids. Which animal is the herbivore and which is the carnivore?

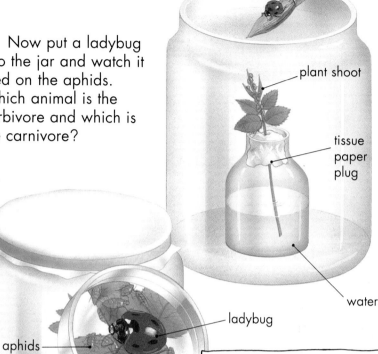

plant shoot

tissue paper plug

water

ladybug

aphids

A Woodland Food Web

This diagram on the left shows "what eats what" in a woodland habitat. Energy for life begins with the Sun. Plants use the energy from sunlight to make food. Herbivores (in the orange band) eat the plants and are then eaten by the carnivores. Try to pick out a simple food chain; for example, an acorn is eaten by a mouse which is then eaten by an owl. Can you work out any other food chains? (Turn to page 32 for some more examples.)

grass

A Delicate Balance

Kestrels are predators of mice —that is, they feed on them. When there are lots of mice, the kestrel has plenty of food and produces many young. But if the mouse population goes down, so does the number of kestrels.

Pollution Problems

One of the many threats to our wildlife is waste. In nature, waste materials such as dead plants and animals are quickly broken down and recycled. But much of the waste we produce is harmful and difficult to get rid of. Harmful waste is called pollution. Some of the most damaging pollution is caused by factories and cars. They produce fumes that turn the rain acid. Acid rain has killed millions of trees. If we want to protect our environment, we must learn to cut down on the amount of pollution we are producing.

You can see waste almost everywhere you look—in the home, on the roads, in cities, and on farms. Garbage is buried in the countryside, liquid waste is poured into rivers and oceans, and harmful fumes are pumped into the air.

acid rain

factory fumes

farming chemicals

garbage

Litter That Kills

Litter can be dangerous to wildlife. Sometimes small animals, such as mice and voles, climb into bottles, only to find they cannot get out again. Without food, they soon starve to death.

liquid waste from factories

transportation fumes

How Can We Help?

- Don't drop litter. It may be a death trap.
- Cut down on pollution by using the car less. Ride a bicycle or walk on short trips.
- If you spot bad pollution, write a letter of complaint to your local government.

Algal Blooms

Sometimes you may find a thick green blanket of algae (tiny plants) floating on a river or pond. This is called an algal bloom. Eventually it leads to the death of fish living in the water. An algal bloom occurs when fertilizers from local farmland drain into a river or pond, causing the algae to grow very fast.

Do it yourself

Find out how polluted your local stream or pond is by discovering which creatures live in the water.

Sweep a dipping net through the water to catch some tiny animals. Use this chart to identify your animals and find out how polluted the water is.

Some animals can only live in unpolluted water. If you find these, you know your water is clean. Others can survive in badly polluted water.

WHAT TO LOOK FOR		
mayfly larva	stone fly larva	No pollution
caddis fly larva	freshwater shrimp	Slight pollution
water louse	bloodworm	Medium pollution
sludgeworm	rat-tailed maggot	Bad pollution
none found		Very bad

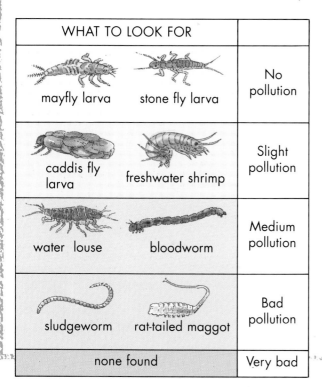

Turn to page 15 to find out how to make and use a dipping net.

Wonderful Woodlands

Your local woodlands are important habitats because they are home to so many different plants and animals. The leaves and branches of the trees form a canopy high above the ground, providing shelter and food for birds and mammals. Leaf litter covers the woodland floor. It is teeming with creatures such as spiders, beetles, thrips, centipedes, and wood lice. When woods are cut down to make way for roads, factories, farms, and expanding towns, all of these wonderful animals lose their homes.

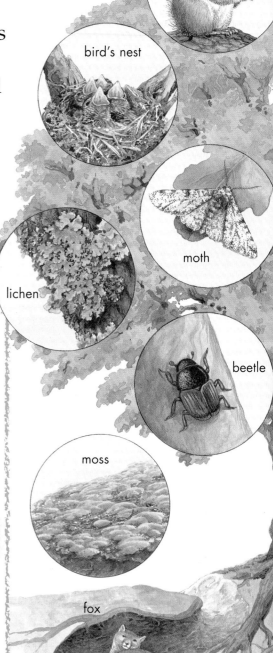

squirrel

bird's nest

moth

lichen

beetle

moss

fox

Do it yourself

Grow a tree from seed.

1. Fill a small flowerpot or yogurt container with potting soil. Make a hole in the soil about 1.5in. deep. Push a seed into the hole and cover it with soil.

2. Put your pot in a warm sunny place and keep the soil damp. By spring, you may have a young sapling. Dig a small hole outside in a shady spot and plant your tree in it, along with its soil.

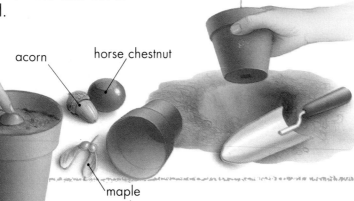

sapling

acorn

horse chestnut

maple seed

woodpecker

caterpillar

nuthatch

This picture shows just a few of the hundreds of different plants and animals that live in an oak tree. Small plants such as mosses and ferns grow on the trunk. Insects move among its branches. Small mammals come to the tree in search of food and shelter. And many birds build their nests in trees.

How Can We Help?

- Plant your own tree (see opposite page).
- Join an organization that plants trees and cares for woodlands.
- If your local woods are under threat, start a petition with family and friends asking your town to save it.

Do it yourself

Do a tree survey to find out as much as you can about a tree near you. Keep all your results in a special book.

1. Take a photograph of your tree in each season. Stand in the same spot each time to get the same view.

2. Collect a winter twig, a spring bud, a summer flower, and a fall fruit or seed.

photographs

3. Find out how old your tree is by measuring around the trunk about 3 feet above the ground. Count one year for every 1 inch you measure.

4. Take leaf and bark rubbings using a wax crayon and paper. Press some leaves in your book as well—one for each season.

5. Use a field guide to identify what kind of plants and animals are living in and around your tree.

leaf rubbing

bark rubbing

Forests in Danger

Trees are very useful plants. As well as being home to a wealth of wildlife, their wood can be used for making paper, for building homes and furniture, and as fuel. Also, when plants make food from sunlight, they use up a gas called carbon dioxide and release the gas oxygen. People breathe in oxygen and breathe out carbon dioxide, and trees help to balance the level of these gases in the air. Yet all around the world, forests are rapidly being destroyed for timber or to grow crops.

More than half the world's rain forests have already been destroyed. If we continue to cut them down, there will be no forests left 50 years from now.

👁 Eye-Spy

Go into each room at home and see how many things you can find that come from trees. Here are some ideas.

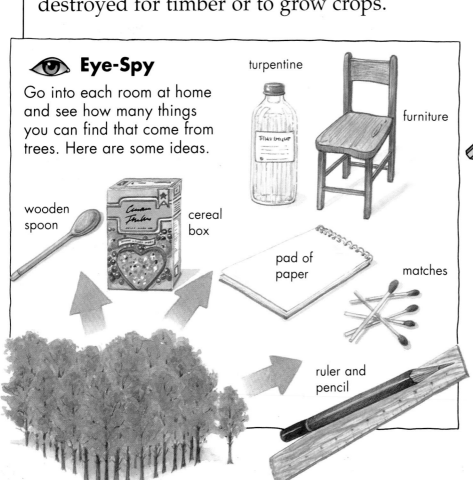

turpentine

furniture

wooden spoon

cereal box

pad of paper

matches

ruler and pencil

Do it yourself

Show that plants give off a gas.

1. Fill a bowl or glass tank with water. Put a glass or jar into the water and tip it up so that all the air escapes.

2. Place some pondweed in the glass without letting any air back in. (You can buy pondweed from a pet shop.)

Drugs from the Forest

Did you know that many of our medicines are made from plants that grow in the rain forest? Drugs made from this rosy periwinkle are used to treat leukemia. Unless we save the remaining rain forests, we will lose many useful plants that could save lives.

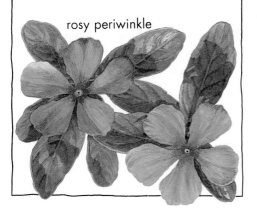

rosy periwinkle

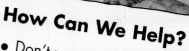

Rain forests are home to at least three-fourths of all the world's wildlife. Millions of different kinds of plant and animal live there, but many of them have not yet been discovered.

How Can We Help?

- Don't waste paper—you are also wasting trees.
- Collect newspapers and cardboard for recycling.
- When people buy new furniture, they should check that it is not made of wood from the rain forests, such as teak and mahogany.

4. Leave the tank for a few days in a warm sunny place. Watch the gas bubbling off the plant and collecting at the top of the glass. This gas is oxygen, produced by the plant as it makes food.

3. Turn the glass upside down in the water and sit it on three small blobs of modeling clay. Make sure you leave a small gap underneath the glass.

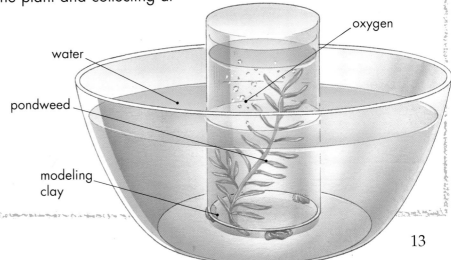

oxygen

water

pondweed

modeling clay

13

Rivers, Ponds, and Lakes

Clean, fresh water is home to a wide variety of wildlife. Animals such as fish, snails, crayfish, and insects live in the water itself, dragonflies and mayflies skim across the surface, water birds live close by, and water plants flourish on the banks. But many of our rivers, ponds, and lakes have become polluted by waste chemicals that pour into them from farms and factories. Sometimes only the hardiest plants and animals survive in the filthy water.

A healthy river is teeming with wildlife living in and around the water. A polluted stretch of river has little life in it. The dirty water often smells and may be full of all kinds of litter. An algal bloom may float on the water's surface.

Fisherman's Threat

Waterbirds sometimes get tangled in fishing lines left on riverbanks by careless fishermen. The birds may die if the line gets too tight around their throats.

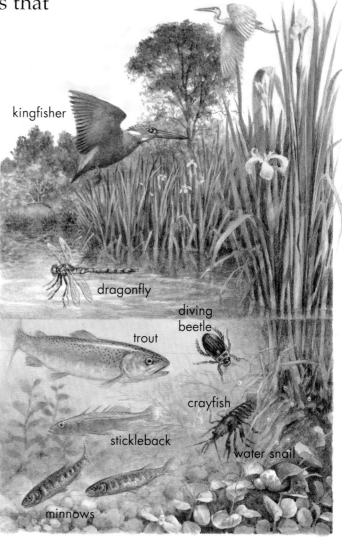

heron

iris

kingfisher

algal bloom

dragonfly

diving beetle

litter

trout

crayfish

stickleback

water snail

minnows

Clean-Up Campaign

Many young people spend some of their spare time helping to clean up their local river or pond, making it much safer for wildlife. Find out if there is a clean-up campaign near you that you can join.

Do it yourself

Make your own pond dipping net.

1. Ask an adult to cut a piece off a metal coat hanger about 28in. long. Bend the wire into a circle leaving 2in. at each end, then poke the ends into a bamboo stick. Tape the ring in place with duct tape.

2. Cut the legs off a pair of panty hose. Sew the cut edges together to make a "bag" out of the waist part.

3. Fold the top edge of the panty hose over the wire and sew it down to hold the bag firmly in place. You are now ready to use your net.

4. Take a large plastic container with you to keep your animals in, plus a magnifying glass. When you have caught some animals in your net, do not pick them up with your fingers—you may squash them. Instead, turn the net inside out and lower it into the water inside the container. Always put the animals back when you have finished looking at them.

coat hanger

tape

top of panty hose

needle and thread

plastic container

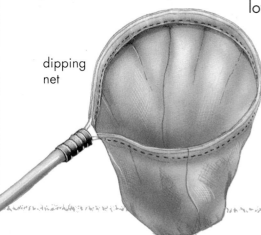

dipping net

magnifying glass

Save Our Seas

Today, our seas are under threat. We rely on the seas to provide us with food, particularly fish. But we are catching far too many fish, so their numbers are going down rapidly. Pollution, too, is a problem. For many years, people thought that getting rid of waste at sea was safe and that it would be quickly diluted. But poisons build up in the water and affect the health of sea animals. All over the world, dolphins and seals are dying from new diseases and fish are found with strange-looking growths on their skin.

Almost three-fourths of the Earth's surface is covered by water. Yet we manage to pollute much of it and make fish stocks dangerously low.

Animals such as dolphins, turtles, and sharks often get caught up in fishing nets. Purse seine nets are like huge bags, whereas drift nets are more like curtains. Both of these nets can be death traps. Long lines are much better because they only catch the fish that are wanted.

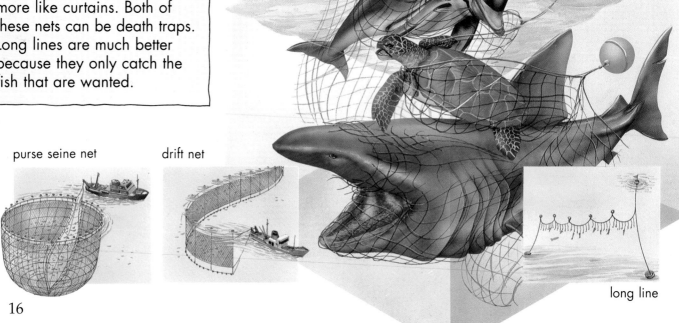

purse seine net

drift net

long line

16

Do it yourself

Do this simple test to see how oil damages a bird's feathers.

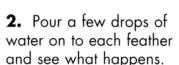

clean feather

oily feather

1. Collect two feathers. Then rub a few drops of bicycle oil or lubricating oil onto one of the feathers using some cotton balls.

2. Pour a few drops of water on to each feather and see what happens.

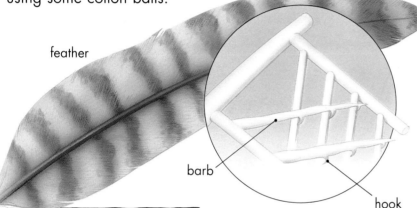

feather

barb

hook

How It Works

The drops of water on the clean feather roll off because the feather is waterproof. Too much oil destroys the waterproofing, so the water soaks into the spoiled feather and spoils its shape. Birds with oily feathers cannot fly or dive and soon die from cold and hunger.

More Things To Try

The barbs of a feather are attached to one another with hooks, rather like Velcro. Oil damages the feathers so that the hooks no longer work and the bird cannot fly.

With a magnifying glass look at the hooks on a feather. Try breaking the hooks apart then joining them up again like a zipper. This effect means that even if the feathers break apart in stormy weather, the bird can always "zip" them up again by preening them into shape.

Oil tankers move millions of tons of oil around the world each year. When there is an accident, oil spills into the sea, where it causes terrible damage to wildlife. Thousands of seabirds may die. If the birds are rescued quickly, the oil can be removed from their feathers by washing them carefully in detergents such as dishwashing liquid.

Farming Takes Over

The number of people in the world has increased rapidly over the last two hundred years, and it is still increasing. All these extra mouths need food to eat, and farming has had to keep up with the demand. Natural habitats are destroyed to make way for huge fields. Chemicals are sprayed onto the fields to increase the yield (output). There are fertilizers to feed the crops and pesticides to kill pests. But these chemicals cause pollution, and pesticides kill more than just the pests.

Free-Range

Many farm animals live indoors, packed together with no room to move. But some farmers let their animals roam free outdoors. These animals are called free-range.

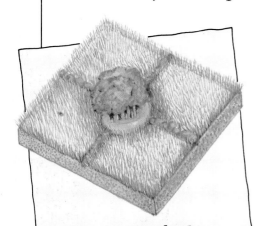

Natural Pockets

To avoid using harmful pesticides, some farmers grow small pockets of woodland in the corners of their fields. Many of the animals that live there feed on the pests.

On a farm, the huge fields are usually planted with a single crop and sprayed with chemicals. Few plants and animals are found living here.

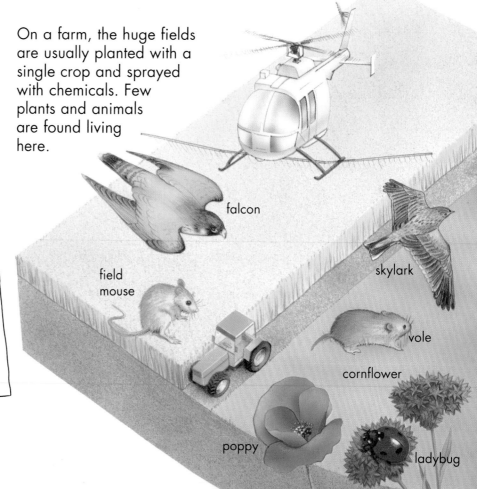

falcon

skylark

field mouse

vole

cornflower

poppy

ladybug

Combine harvesters are used to cut down crops. But they also destroy small animals that get in their way.

In comparison to farmland, natural meadows and woodlands are rich in wildlife. It is important to protect these habitats.

falcon

frog

obit

butterfly

primrose

daisy

Do it yourself

Worms are farmers' friends. As they burrow through the soil, they mix it all up and let air into it. This helps to keep the soil healthy. You can watch worms at work by making a worm farm.

1. Take a large glass jar and fill it with three layers of different soils—gravel or sand, mud from a stream, and ordinary soil will do.

2. Add a layer of leaves. Then put four or five worms on top.

3. Wrap black paper around your worm farm to keep it dark and make sure the soil is kept moist. Check it after a day or two to see what has happened.

City Living

Modern cities are really jungles of concrete and asphalt. Yet a city habitat is very different from a natural habitat such as woods. Despite this, wildlife can be found even in the center of the world's busiest cities. Animals are attracted to cities because there is a vast and never-ending supply of free food, such as the food that gets thrown out with our garbage. Many birds and mammals make their homes in parks and tree-lined roads, whereas animals such as rats and mice live beneath the cities in the sewers and drains.

👁 Eye-Spy

You have to look quite carefully to spot some city dwellers. Old walls may be home to a host of tiny plants and animals. How many creatures can you find living on a wall?

Cities can be home to some unlikely guests including moose, monkeys, raccoons, and foxes. Others animals, such as rats and mice, are more common inhabitants.

moose in Canadian and Scandinavian towns

pigeons

fox

rats

vervet monkeys in towns in Africa

mice

Attract birds to your backyard or school ground by putting out bird food.

To make a coconut cake, melt 8oz. of lard or suet. Mix in 1lb of raisins, peanuts, bread and cake crumbs, sunflower seeds, and oatmeal. Put the mix into half a coconut shell and let it set before you hang it up outside.
   Make a string of peanuts in the shell by threading the nuts together using a large needle and strong thread.

storks often nest on rooftops in northern European towns

Polar bears are among the largest visitors to towns—and the most dangerous! Many are attracted by the free supply of food to be found in garbage dumps.

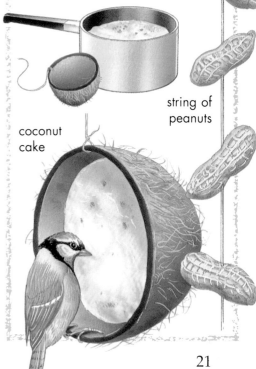

string of peanuts

coconut cake

raccoons are found in cities in the U.S.A.

Life on the Highways

Roads reach almost everywhere. Roadsides are often planted with grass and trees to look attractive and control erosion. Although there is pollution from car fumes, the roadsides are usually free from harmful pesticides—and have formed homes for many plants and animals. The plants attract insects, birds, and mammals. Some birds feed on dead insects that bounce off car windshields. Other birds and foxes feed on animals that are killed on the road.

kestrel

fox

Beware!

Special road signs are used to warn drivers about animals crossing the road. This safeguards the animals, but also prevents drivers from having accidents.

Roadsides attract many plants and animals that do not mind living so close to traffic.

Save a Toad

Every spring, toads travel to their breeding ponds. They often have to cross roads, and many get killed. Now, people help toads by carrying them safely across the roads.

bee

rabbit

butterfly

hedgehog

vole

Do it yourself

Make a highway habitat mobile.

1. Trace the shapes off this page and transfer them onto cardboard. You will need one hawk, four mice, and two of each of the fruits. Cut your shapes out.

2. Paint or color the shapes on both sides. Use a felt-tip pen to add the details.

3. Ask an adult to help you pierce holes in your shapes as marked on the pattern. Then string your mobile together using a needle and thick thread. Follow the diagram on the right to see where each of the pieces should go.

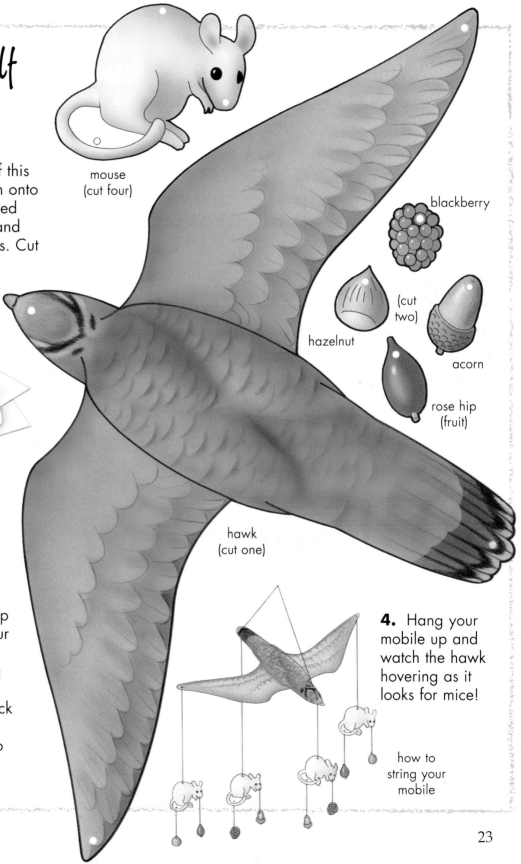

mouse
(cut four)

blackberry

(cut
two)

hazelnut

acorn

rose hip
(fruit)

hawk
(cut one)

4. Hang your mobile up and watch the hawk hovering as it looks for mice!

how to
string your
mobile

23

Hunting and Collecting

People have hunted animals for food and skins for thousands of years. Today, animals are hunted for sport or for their horns, tusks, bones, or fur. Hunting and collecting threatens the survival of many creatures. There are now laws to protect some animals, such as the law banning the trade in elephant ivory. Sadly, animals such as big cats are still hunted, even though they are protected by law. The poachers can make lots of money by selling their fur.

 Eye-Spy

When you are on vacation, look out for souvenirs and objects in the stores that are made from wild animals, such as ivory ornaments, crocodile skin bags, coral, sponges, and shells. Would you want to buy any of these?

Elephant tusks are made of ivory, which is very valuable. Poachers have killed thousands of elephants in Africa, but trade in ivory is now banned and the poaching has almost stopped.

Do it yourself

Hunting animals may be cruel but tracking them is not, and it can be great fun.

Next time you go for a walk, look for any tracks or signs left by animals. See if you can figure out what kind of animals they were. Things to look for include bits of fur, feathers, footprints, leftover food, animal footpaths in the grass, and droppings.

How Can We Help?

- Don't collect birds' eggs, butterflies, wildflowers, or any other living thing.
- If you collect wild animals such as snails or pond creatures to study, keep them only for a short time and always return them to their natural habitat afterward.
- Don't kill animals just because you don't like them—spiders, moths, ants, and slugs are just as important as bigger animals.

Big cats such as leopards and tigers have been killed for their beautiful fur. Many people believe fur looks better worn by the cat—not when worn by a person.

 rat prints

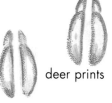
squirrel prints (back paws)

hazelnut eaten by a squirrel

hazelnut eaten by a mouse

fur caught on barbed wire

pine cone eaten by a squirrel

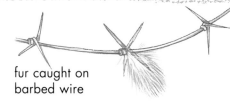
fox droppings

deer droppings   rabbit droppings

mouse prints

deer prints

Small mammals have their own particular way of eating nuts and pine cones, so look out for these signs.

You can usually recognize animal droppings by their shape. Also look for fur caught on barbed wire.

Each animal has its own set of footprints. They often show up best in mud or snow. See if you can find any of these footprints.

fox prints

Endangered Wildlife

Many plants and animals have disappeared completely from Earth. That is, they have become extinct. Sometimes this happens naturally. Dinosaurs may have died out because of a sudden change in climate. But many species are now extinct because of humans. Destruction of habitat is the biggest threat to wildlife. It has made animals, such as the giant panda, become endangered—that is there are only a few thousand individuals, or even fewer, left in the world.

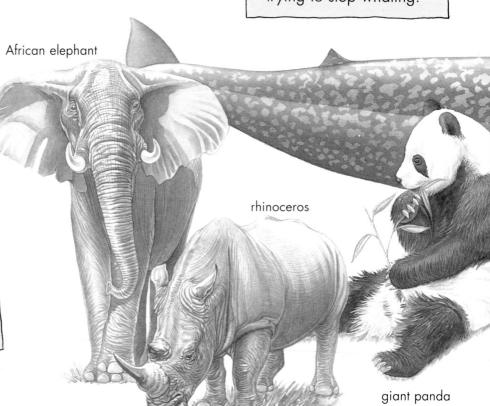

Special organizations such as Greenpeace try to protect endangered animals. Here, they are trying to stop whaling.

African elephant

rhinoceros

giant panda

Extinct!

The dodo was a large flightless bird that lived in Mauritius. An easy catch for sailors, the last one was killed in 1700.

Running Wild

Wolves were once a common sight in the United States and Europe. But they caught sheep and cattle, so they were shot by farmers. They are now being reintroduced to places where they once roamed wild.

Countryside Code

Many of us can do little to help tigers and whales, but we can all help to conserve wildlife by following a few simple rules when we go into nature reserves and parks.

Many well-known animals are endangered. If these animals are not protected, and their habitats conserved, they may soon disappear forever. Imagine what the world would be like without tigers, elephants, pandas, and whales!

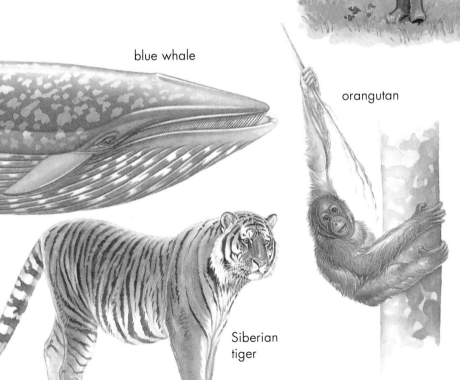

blue whale

orangutan

Siberian tiger

- Do not pick any wild-flowers, even if there are plenty of them.
- Keep to the paths so you do not trample wildflowers.
- Keep your dog on a leash if there are animals or nesting birds around.
- Close gates so that farm animals do not escape.

Zoos Today

For a long time, zoos were simply places where animals were kept in small cages to entertain the public. The modern zoo, however, has a far more important role. Many zoos keep endangered animals. This is often the only way to stop an animal becoming extinct. The zoos breed them in special enclosures. Eventually, they may be able to release some of the animals back into the wild.

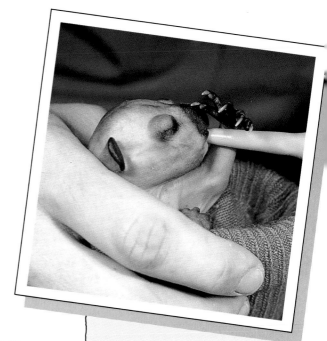

Sometimes a mother animal abandons her baby, so zookeepers have to rear it by hand. This baby koala is only a few days old.

Modern zoos have large enclosures where the animals can live together. The brown bear above is catching salmon from a stream in its enclosure. Older zoos have small brick cages. Animals have little room to move around and are often kept on their own for all of their lives.

Pets and Performers

These days people keep many exotic pets, such as snakes, monkeys, and spiders. In the past, it was also common to keep performing animals to entertain. Dolphins, elephants, lions, and many others were trained to do tricks. But this became unpopular with the public because the animals were often cruelly treated.

Performing Bears

Once, bears were often chained up and made to perform on the streets for money. This now happens in only a few places.

finch

colobus monkey

tarantula

parrot

python

Many pets come from far-away places. They are often caught in the wild and transported across the world to be sold in pet shops. A large number of them may die during the long journey.

Do it yourself

Keep some pet snails for a few days.

1. Find a tin lid. Cut a strip of acetate 12in. wide and long enough to line the lid. Put the acetate in the lid as shown and tape it in place. Make an acetate lid to fit and pierce holes in it.

2. Put soil, rocks, leaves, and twigs into the snail tank, then add your snails. Tape the acetate lid on top. Be sure to keep your tank damp and give your snails plenty of leaves to eat.

acetate

tin lid

tape

rocks

Make a Nature Reserve

It is easy to attract wildlife into our yards, especially birds. Climbing plants and bushes give the birds shelter, an upturned garbage can lid makes a good birdbath, and plants such as teasels and globe thistles provide food. Grow grass long if you want to attract insects—even a pile of logs and flowerpots can be home to a surprising number of animals.

Attracting Butterflies

- Buddleia, poppies, sedum, scabious, and lavender are all good for attracting butterflies, which feed off their sweet nectar.
- Ragwort and cabbages are good food plants for caterpillars.

Turn a corner of your yard into a nature reserve. Build a pond to attract a wealth of wildlife, from snails and dragonflies to frogs, newts, and maybe the occasional duck. Piles of logs will house insects, centipedes, spiders, and toads. And a compost heap for kitchen waste and grass cuttings will become home to worms and toads.

Do it yourself

Build a yard pond to attract water creatures.

1. Dig a hole in the ground about 20in. deep and 5ft. across. Gently slope the sides of the hole down to the bottom.

2. Line the hole with sand (about 2.5in. deep) or with layers of newspaper. Lay a sheet of thick plastic, about 6ft. square, on top.

3. Anchor the sheet with rocks around the edges as shown.

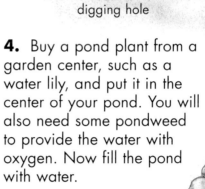

digging hole

rocks

thick plastic

4. Buy a pond plant from a garden center, such as a water lily, and put it in the center of your pond. You will also need some pondweed to provide the water with oxygen. Now fill the pond with water.

5. Dip your net in the pond every week to see what new animals are living there. Remember to keep the water level high in dry weather.

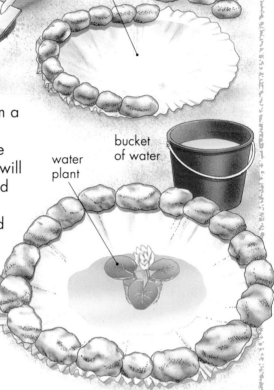

water plant

bucket of water

More Things to Try

If you do not have a yard, you may still be able to put out a window box filled with flowers to attract wildlife. Plants such as night-scented stock, sweet william, thyme, petunia, and candytuft provide plenty of color and scent, and will attract many insects, especially butterflies.

Index

Food Chains (page 6-7)
Here are some more food chains for you to follow. Stinging nettle to caterpillar to thrush; grass to deer to human; hazelnut to squirrel to fox; blackberry to finch to owl; dandelion to snail to thrush.